VISIONS FOR THE NIGHT

POEMS BY KEN HADA

VISIONS FOR THE NIGHT

Cover Image: *event horizon 2* by Steven Schroeder
Book Design: Rowan Kehn

ISBN: 979-8-9868994-6-6

Turning Plow Press

I yet have visions for the night.
And for the day faint visions there is store.

John Keats
Ode on Indolence

for Arlo Wren Hada

CONTENTS

Foreword

Ken Hada is a poet who comfortably rejects clear boundaries, although his work would seem filled with them: light and dark, the four seasons, beginnings and endings, youth and old age. But these are mostly offered as moments of transition, signaled by unexpected sights, sounds, whispers, songs— human or bird produced—that speak out of the coming light or coming darkness. Dawns are equally beginnings and endings; dusk is still defused with light. For example, the poem "This Mercy Light Angel Pink" begins with "This mercy light angel pink/softly glows and then/slowly gives way to the broad/full light of day," and ends with ambiguous interplay of light and dark: for in "the pink of morning/is the blood of life/pulsing through the dark."

One might just as easily say that Hada is primarily a poet of ambiguities, especially of the sort we find in the Romantic tradition. It is only proper that the title of this newest collection borrows a line from Keats—whose term *negative capability*, as Keats says, occurs "when man is capable of being in uncertainties, Mysteries, doubts, without any irritable reaching after fact & reason...," where, for a "great poet, the sense of Beauty overcomes every other consideration." Hada is indeed a poet similarly "capable of being in uncertainties." In "Hidden Creek," ostensibly about a creek that is concealed by tall grass, "You'd never know it's there/until you've stepped in it—/but there it is - springing/from somewhere, going someplace," and, "Like so many things hidden,/you never know them until/you're in them." What are those "things hidden"? What is it we are meant to "know"? The facts of the creek subtly turn toward the negative, as Keats intends the term: a space, a mystery, that opens up beneath us, and we find ourselves "in it."

Henry James, in *The Art of the Novel*, makes a similar distinction between reality (Keats' "fact & reason") and romance. "The real," James argues, "represents to my perception the things we cannot possibly *not* know, sooner or later, in one way or another...The romantic stands, on the other hand, for the things that, with all the facilities in the world, all the wealth and all the courage and all the wit and all the adventure, we never *can* directly know; the things that can reach us only through the beautiful circuit and subterfuge of our thought and our desire."

Both Keats and James are expressing the effects of the Romantic sensibility on the audience, but they are also describing the complex, mysterious processes of artistic perception and creation. Donald Hall, in an interview with Bill Moyers for the 1993 documentary, *A Life Together: Donald Hall and Jane Kenyon*, reads his marvelous poem, "White Apples," an elegy to his father. When Moyers says that the enigmatic line "white apples and the taste of stone" reminded him of "a cemetery and white apples that are sometimes on the frieze of some of the big mausoleums," Hall, surprised and clearly delighted, suddenly recalls that he wrote that poem while living near a cemetery, but then adds, "And it's not logical. It's not syntactical, it's not logical." And then he says this:

> A poem so often, obviously and correctly, pointing south and at the same time something under it is going north...There is ambivalence coded into it. You are aware of one half of it and unaware of another half which contradicts the first half, and they're both true. They're both true. They're both there. In order to write it, you cannot be aware of the second part. You couldn't write it if you were. This has been true again and again for poems of mine. And then later I've discovered that I was not only saying north, I was saying south as well, not knowing it.

In Hada's "Directions," the speaker complains, "I want to know and ignorance makes me mad.//Ignorance and inquisitiveness—and the importance/that accompanies these forces—push me/forward, pull me backwards.//I am going two directions at once." And, like the nightingale in Keats' ode, the speaker reveals, "I hear a bird chirp in darkness./Is it a wren, or something else,/something unknown?" That "unknown," which is a frequent trope in Hada's work, resounds like Keats' "Forlorn!" bringing the poet back to the reality of his life, just as occurs in Hada's poem when the speaker finds himself again in "dark moments,/in this contorted abyss, this eternal chasm/between daylight and death."

I would not claim "Directions" is a deliberate, conscious reference to "Ode to a Nightingale," but the tenor of this poem, and many others in this collection, clearly evokes that sublime undercurrent, the northward movement, as Hall labels it, of which even the poet is perhaps unaware. It is indeed that "beautiful circuit and subterfuge" of which Henry James writes that informs and infuses these powerful visions for the night.

Paul Bowers
Turning Plow Press

DEFLECTING AS I RECEIVE

This Mercy Light Angel Pink

This mercy light angel pink
softly glows and then
slowly gives way to the broad,
full light of day.

The long, dark night
tossing and turning with a mind
that won't turn off

until Tuesday morning
when the mercy light angel pink
exposes the world, and I
begin to see, and color
returns like breath

in measured counts – my feet follow
in awkward rhythm,
the cadence eventually established
and with unspoken praise
I walk in mercy

trying to forget, and for a while
believe all those bumps
in the night were just noise
without meaning

and the pink of morning
is the blood of life
pulsing through the dark.

Thunder Sounds Morning Sky Alive

Thunder sounds morning sky alive.
Lightning flashes – and for a moment
the dark is parted and a line
between *Then* and *Now* is clarified.

I am reminded of what I am not.

There is no feeling of loss or hope,
no call for my response.

I only watch the morning sky divide.

Rain follows to wash all noise away,
except its own sensation.

I am passive as stone.
Sound bounces off me – bounces
between the felt and the imagined –
the way light has come and gone.

A Solitary Cottonwood

It stands at the end of a draw
so far removed from the rest
of everything.

Its isolation commands
an uncertain response –
the appearance of peace conflated
with its odd independence
complicates, frightens.

Hermit-like, it discomforts,
causes unsolicited reflection –
a rustic truth compromised
by the consolation of lies.

Hidden Creek

The grass along its edge
protects it from view,
moving toward Cottonwoods
at the end of the draw.

You'd never know it's there
until you've stepped in it –
but there it is – springing
from somewhere, going
someplace, fulfilling its part
on this ball of water –
part in the greater whole.

Like so many things hidden,
you never know them until
you're in them, and afterward,
come away with the thing
called *Experience* –
mislabeling them *good* or
bad – when, maybe,
it's just our own little part
in that bigger whole.

Rivers

Rivers never run straight.
They always bend.
Eventually, the water
turns your way.

If you flow with the current,
long enough, don't fight
the flow, but receive
the assault, navigate
the torrents, hang on
through the upheaval,
you will find yourself

and the struggle
through which you
have paddled with patience
will diminish – you
will survive, you will be
changed for the better.

And like all survivors,
you will have stories
to tell – you will do
what you have not yet
imagined.

You will be a hero
in your own little drama.
Even tragedy
has its legacy – and the art
that results will claim
you for its own.

The Pulse of Morning

A beaver slides
into the water's edge
in morning sun,
cruises the placid lake,
cutting a wake,
then ducks down under
for an invisible
distance before surfacing
at the opposite shore.
Moving as instinct
directs, he does what he does
without reflection, but
with Edenic stealth, follows
the pulse of morning.

This Pecan Tree

This Pecan Tree
is now twenty years
in the ground,
higher than my roof.

Fully leafed in May,
birds shelter here.

But once in an October past,
before its full green self,
a Road Runner climbed
its rough branches,
sat like a pirate waiting,
then fell flying
onto an unsuspecting victim.

I witnessed this drama –
the arduous climb,
the clandestine perch,
the terrible assault

and I thought how strange,
how beautiful, how brutal.

The History We Are

Hear the crow call.
See the crow flap
against morning light –
wrens secluded
in wintered branches,
a jogger in purple
moves around the lake
in careful trot,
two mallards in shallows.

The sycamores are white.
The cedars are green.
There is no breeze.
Brown oak leaves cling
to what once was.
Everything hangs on
to what has been
while the crow voices
the history we are.

After the Wind

It blew all night, hard
from due north
piercing
my bedroom wall,
an old quilt
tucked to my neck,
hearing
the relentless howling,
wondering
what animals feel,
knowing
in ways they do not,
yet sharing
a similar skin.

This calm morning,
aglow with gold sun,
confronts me
and I emerge
from slumber
in a somber mood.

Soon birdsong fills the air
and reflection
starts to shape me
into something alive,
confused with breath –
conspiring memory
with moments
too fresh for words.

What on earth,
I wonder, can anything mean
beyond survival –
nothing more than seeds
driven by violent air,
landing somewhere in exile,
stranded in beauty
so easily forgotten,
scattered onto a prairie
we sometimes call a garden.

In the Pastel Glow of Sundown

Birds sitting on bare limbs
are colorless, dark
ink spots
on canvas too vast
for comfort.

Holding tight to branches,
their shapes
seem like statues of stone.
Nightfall brings us
together.

Their songs diminish.
Sky colors blend
into horizon
and trees grow dense
with the dusk.

Thoughts come and go.
I wait on a feeling
to move me
indoors, after this
exhibit

of painted sky, birds
and trees.
The sky loses its glow.
I try to believe
in sunrise.

Red Smoke is a Broken Window

Red smoke is a broken window
opening on an animal eternity.

Fields on fire in March –
wind like Devil's breath

stokes, pushes, consumes.
Only the biggest bones will be

found after fire burns itself away –
after the Beast has been satisfied.

Look! Look out. Look in –
this terror is nothing –

the only thing is instinct –
a pistol shot fired – and I run

and I run – and I run – but fire
is fleet of foot,
and the animal I am –

only flesh and bone.

Anticipation

I am awake with the morning.
Our conversation may soon begin
but first we acknowledge
each other, our presence
coming together
with a shy sleepy nod,
a stretch or two,
a leftover yawn –
our mutual gazing,
taking the measure of the other –
then deciding we
are not so different –
the morning and I – awakening
while filtered sun warms
our breath, stoking
life's embers from dark night
just passed.

Our common bond established,
now we are ready to talk,
to hear what each has to say.

Our partnership, born in silence,
springing slowly in what
we share – old dreams
to turn death into green –
the slumber washing away
through teary eyes blinking.

March Morning

I'm watching wind wisp
across water,
north wind blowing steady,
the water moving north to south,
the sun rising in the east.

It's early morning, it's cool,
but spring is on the way.
Some days I feel like I am a seed
blown by this wind,
and wonder where I will land.

I'm learning to trust wind.
There's not much you can do but allow
yourself to be taken to places
you don't know, surrender
to the elements.

I come from elements,
and so I will return.
In this meantime
I try to stand, try to work,
try to be good,
and there's some comfort
knowing, however it turns out,
in the end I may be something useful –
a chair, a blade, an old song.

Only the Wind

Morning catches me unaware.
Old self-loathing returns.
Only the wind is saving me,
blowing strong so early,
and the Yellow-Billed Cuckoo
cackling – and Carolina Wrens calling.

I notice a June bug, wholly intact
but dead, in the bottom
of an empty flower pot where rings
of rainwater ended its life.

Why couldn't it simply fly away?
Was rain that restraining?
The nourishing gift of heaven
sometimes falls hard on us,
grounding bugs to death – something
I notice, something I think about –
maybe a little too much.

Directions

Before even the turkey gobbles from its roost,
or the morning rooster crows,
I walk the silent hillside in darkness.

Like a fool, I have no fear.

I am fueled by anger and curiosity –
two emotions that have marked my life.

I want to know and ignorance makes me mad.

Ignorance and inquisitiveness – and the impotence
that accompanies these forces – push me
forward, pull me backwards.

I am going two directions at once.

I hear a bird chirp in darkness.
Is it a wren, or something else,
something unknown?

Do sounds differ before daylight?

Jimenez says *You find in solitude
only what you take to it.*

Much of my existence is solitary –
maybe too much, some may say,
but I don't know what else to do,
how other to be

except to own myself – complete
and confined – in these dark moments,
in this contorted abyss, this eternal chasm
between daylight and death.

A Strange Weed

When daylight filters
through morning clouds
and birdsong
accompanies your vision,
you sit still, feel
breeze on bare arms,
foregoing breakfast
except for a cup of coffee
to wake you,
to welcome life
budding and blossoming –
setting aside the past
for a few moments,
refusing the future
while morning arrives
and you realize
things that matter –
things unspoken, things
heard, seen, felt –
what it must be like
to be a strange weed
in a fallen world,
recovering – unaware
of an audience –
unconsumed –
moments of being
that make you more
than human –
a friend to yourself
looking with longing
into that which mirrors
you – rich soil

beneath you, patient
as a saint.

Born Under a Full Moon

Inside the Austin hospital
nurses and doctors
and all the rest perform
their services – professional,
confident – a system
our science makes possible.

But outside a full moon
is watching you – a great eye
in the sky – and sitting
on my deck in Oklahoma,
having witnessed your first cry,
your contentment in the arms
of Mom and Dad, my heart
brimming with gratitude
I see the ambient light
caressing the oaks –
a few stars giving way
to moonlight's triumphant blaze.

I want you to know you
were born under a good moon,
and I pray you will always know
the rhythms of our universe –
that no matter how technical
we become, how far from home
your life will take you,
that mystery remains –
and that reflection in your eyes
says more than any scientist
could know, more
than any poet could conjure.

The depth of feeling, the Eros
of life – passion sprouting
around us like greening grass
and morning birdsong
is your birthright.

You came to us under a full moon,
and may you always know
the balance of life –
how natural we are,
how mysterious, mythical –
glorified in that which
we can never explain.

This Miraculous World

I call it miraculous.
I don't know a better word
to describe the cold rain
in October – the way it pounds
the prairie, the way it penetrates
old ground and an old soul.
I hear it, watch it, feel it
in the core of my being
and admit I have nothing
to do with it, and very little to say
about my own sense of self
in seasonal adjustment –
how my survival is not much
to be considered in this falling,
this time when everything slows
and I am but a passive observer.
I survey the sky, smell the soil,
realize the grandeur of life
is beyond my grasp, its subtlety
moving through me.
I am a songbird snuggled in cedar –
the emptiness of it all filling the void
I can hardly name, the mundane
demanding quiet attention –
the profound otherness of everything.

The Peace that Morning Brings

Sometimes Heaven's eye is too hot.
Sometimes the abyss of Earth seems to swallow you.

But other times, morning sun calms the tattered soul

     and the troubles of life fade
     for a while - residual peace falls
     like birdsong on a hillside
     and your true selves are restored
     and you know what is beyond naming -
     the feeling of life well-lived.

     The breeze comforts, displaces storms past -
     the ugly history, the lonely road of deceit.

Sometimes an orchestra plays full - the sounds offering

     the good, the beautiful and the just - these
     ideals you can never disregard
     mindful that the human cause continues
     and the Divine drama resolves itself in your hearts

     and your mind rests - the leaves are green,
     the swaying grass bows in applause,
     cheering you as you walk days and nights of faith
     filling you, renewing Grace.

Even the aging seem to be children again, wrapped in love

     carried by a parent who gives everything
     and you are transformed, moving past fear
     comforted in this season of hope.

The gifts of friends and family finding you –

the voice of God, approving.

Deep Purple Sky

A blanket covers the green
prairie – stillness –
occasional soft thunder,
soft sprinkles, a soft

morning – it's too dark
for the yellow flowers to open.
It's too dark to see
beyond edges.

Deep purple sky covers
everything – trees hold their breath,
but a few birds bounce
between branches.

We are subjects in a painting
the Dutch Masters would envy.
Nothing moves much
but invisible energy.

This is a good time
for coffee and reflection,
though thoughts
struggle to clarify.

Senses are being tuned –
a cosmic orchestra
preparing to play –
adagio.

Bent Cedars

Cedars bent with ice
the morning after freezing rain,
limbs bowed, frozen –
in timeless portrait,
as if that is all.

Brown dead grass –
crystalized – crunches
beneath my boots.

The faceless sky waits.

In this frozen moment,
it is not easy to believe.
This frozen truth

> like the heart of one
> who looks to lowly cedar
> for inspiration

> like the feet of one
> who walks where summer grass
> once swayed in sustaining,
> soothing breeze

> one who mistakes *Now*
> for *Time Immemorial*
> while death clustered crisp

> takes me to a place
> where life aches on hold

something only the dormancy
of faith can withstand –
something ultimate –
the certain uncertainty,
the uncertain certainty

until a return, when limbs
stand upright,
and we walk away
from winter.

Dark Cold Rain

The sun will be slow in coming today.
Rain splatters my roof.
I set my book aside,
pick up my cigar and listen.
What I hear is nothing new,
but it seems new. Always,
it seems new.

The first rainy dawn must have felt like this.
Before light arrives, before night ends.

I'm thinking whatever thoughts come
my way – there is no order
I could know – seems like a script
was written long ago by some author
I can't imagine.

How odd to be a minor character
in some cosmic play, with nothing to do
but listen to dark cold rain – dark
cold rain – waiting silently for a world
to turn, a plot to twist, consume me
in my little role toward some sense
of ending – nothing essential,
eternal, or exceptional.

So much is ordinary.

Maybe art can make the ordinary extraordinary.
Maybe an artist has something worthy to offer.

The lights flicker. The tip of my cigar glows.

Dark cold rain is everywhere.
Dark cold rain is everything.

Despite the Rain

Singing birds come to life
as thunder sounds,
clouds darken.

Rain is coming
in a matter of minutes.
The closer the rain,

the more birds I hear –
at least sixteen different voices.
The closer the rain

the more they sing
like a choir, or rather
an orchestra

against the dull groan
of approaching thunder.
I guess they're happy –

maybe nervous –
I don't know why or even what
but suddenly the timber

is full of sound.
A breeze stirs, rain
is coming. Soon

darkness will return.
Rain will fall.
Some will sing

even in the rain.
Some will sing
despite the rain.

The Shadowed Moon

Stained with dark clouds,
a remnant of light
through Oak limbs
pointing skyward, leafless –
ghostlike.

Soundless prairie, patient
hillside, where most life
now sleeps enclosed in darkness,
I look through the trees
to partial light.

In something of a trance,
I stand arrested
by the dismal glow
covering the land unseen.

Alone with the moon,
its dutiful orbit
reflects half-known truths
that move us – if only we might see.

Are shadows a gift?

Interrupted light is still light.

A mask never fully hides a face –
a face betrayed by wearing a mask,
the one posing in disguise,
who first must hide himself.

Are shadows evil? Are they good?

Just? Beautiful? What would Plato say?

How about Keats?
His melancholy is mine as well.

His indolence, stoked by fear, is a flame
unquenchable, even as the half-moon,
dull but persistent, speaks
of more than mere mechanization.

The part informs the whole,
tells me how incomplete I am,
makes me wonder if completeness is possible –
should even be desired.

Shadows concealing the moon
conceal me, and oddly soothe me.

I guess that feels close enough to right –
maybe more than I have a right to know.

Who am I to enter this secret vigil,
this shroud of being,
this fact of life teetering
on the edge of death?

With the Rain

Doubts are not deleted
but may be dispersed.
Splatters from above
suspend the exigencies
of things unknown.

With rain, Time slows down,
and that is reason enough
to stop, to rethink
that which so easily besets me.

The pasture is soaked.
Like the *Dao*, water
follows a course I know
only afterward.

After the rain, work
will resume with hope
and fear, but with rain
I laugh with the world.

With the rain I fear
nothing, believe
everything. I am
an Oak leaf deflecting
as I receive.

THE WAY A SPARROW PECKS AT THE DUST

Welcome

I am the cellar blue,
a low grass moan
knee-high, hoppy.

A place children
hide and seek,
where Grandma prays

and a bottle of shine
sits dust-covered
in a corner.

You remember
the surface. Some
forgive. Some forget

but truth hides
where lies sing lullabies –
that's the way

of a masked life –
a misunderstood
presence

magnified in turmoil
when my voice
crescendos

when despair's choking
stormy clouds
thicken the air –

but I also know
the shelter of darkness
and invite you in –

a persistent welcome.

This Morning, After Rain

The sun meanders
like a child
late for school.

Light casually lifts
a dark prairie,
a breeze stirs.

Some days are bright
instantly, warm
sun glowing

colors resplendent,
air thick as soup
in a small bowl.

But today is not
that kind of day.
Rain slowly drained

moves to the east
leaving soaked ground,
clouds slowly rise

a curtain opening
a play when some
of the children

will take their marks
having learned lines
in the dark.

Allusions

Walden is no escape today.
I can't see the green trees
in the yellow sun
for the bristling water.

If Emerson is right, where
is the consolation?
I wish I had Emily's subtle sass.
I've lost Whitman's expansive vision.

Today, I feel more like Hart Crane
looking at a bridge
I'm not sure I can cross.

Contradictions

I am new and I am old.
I am weak and I am bold.

I have what I lack
and lack what I have.

I know what I know;
I am ignorant of the rest.

I am empty; I am full.

I am swimming in doubt.
I am drowning in certainty.

I am grounded in hope.
I am flying in fear.

You know me as I am.
You know me as I was.

Everything's the same
because everything has changed.

Sisters

Lust drunk on peach gorgeous
women with gardens
smeared beneath the heaves
like Mother Eve innocently
gathering, playing – her days
filled with undiluted sweetness –
an eternal hope lingering
in the female heart to be free
from blame, to be pure
as air, despite toxic voices
since the beginning exiling
her ways. Now, beneath fig
leaves, her sisters taste the drink
of distorted history.

Brothers

You were deader there
than in a crypt, eddying
in the River of Life
polluted because you
listened to the wrong voices,
doubted Nature's truth,
surrendered to the plow –
haunted by Paradise –
exiled in heart and place –
harnessed by labor's
cursed blessing – trying
to control emptiness
you fear to know – lost
order, destined to death.

Sisyphus Goes Paddling

His kayak bounces on waves.
The wind has its own chaotic mind.
His rowing is futile.
He cannot order his course.

He sets the paddle
across the bow, tightens
his hold on the handles,
settles into his seat.

All his progress drifts away,
driven by hostile air.
The shore slips farther from view.
The rising depths splash
him with abusive laughter,
mocking his humiliation.

He could capsize.
He could drown.

But he'll probably survive
this cruel crossing,
and with heightened fear
and forgotten hope
do nothing.

Nothing can be done
until the force finishes with him.
Then he'll return to rowing
across the deep,
retracing his loss –

the silhouetted distant shore
he had not fathomed –
a sense of ending
unresponsive
to disappointment,
unrepentant,
despite his devotion.

Joan Baez in the Morning

I'm not sure where I am.
It's still dark outside –
springtime temperatures
and pollen-filled breeze –
and Joan Baez dreaming
about St. Augustine:
She *bows her head and cries*

while I am also reading
Charles Simic, and I am
not sure where I am.

Two voices clashing
like waves against the shore.

Definitions of Art may
be debated, but the electricity
can't be denied.

Some of us'll stand up to meet you
on your crossroads, says Dylan,
and in our journeys, the voices
tell of death, fragmented
like broken limbs fallen
after the storm, or egg shells
shattered on the breakfast bar.

Simic says his *guardian angel*
is afraid of the dark,
but then who believes
a *sleepy little girl with glasses*?

Minor poets indeed!
Our time has come.
We just have to get out of bed
and live the darkness.

Facing the Wind

Green grass and green trees –
and the wind.

Grandma used to say
with her unbridled optimism:
We always have a nice breeze out here.

Out here, in western Oklahoma
where only barbed-wire
and the occasional Cottonwood
break the winds
coming from the south (hot
as hell), and the north (cold
as Mars), and the west (surly
as a coiled rattlesnake).

Out here, she lived with wind
as common as breakfast.

I remember, as a boy, helping her
get the evening milking done
(the men were in harvest).
Storm clouds were brewing, wind
was raucous, the cows were nervous,
but we got them stanchioned,
and by hand tried to fill the pails
with pure white milk despite
their feet stomping, heads jerking,
tails swishing our faces – a foam
of red dust settling on the milk.

Out here, she lived and died,
never surrendering to wind,
even when the '47 tornado
pulled her baby from her arms
and she awoke the next morning
in the hospital – that
was just something to face.

Facing the wind – it's still
the best option – in green times
or hard-baked brown.

Like dutiful cows at milking time,
life goes on – we do what must be done
until we all go to a grave – buried
beneath springtime green,
or yellow Cottonwoods in fall –
the living and the dead –
facing the wind forever together.

Witness

An antlered deer
and his doe cross the road
almost giddy with rut.

City workers take
Christmas down.
White ducks stand

in the road. Church people
peddle Gospel
to no one passing by.

The water sits tight
like a lid. Rising sun
sparkles and cars

drift slowly into morning.
A pine tree twists
in its moment

of grace. Night secrets
linger for anyone
who takes time

to look – and one day
leaves will return,
and separate

the buck from the doe.
Decorations will be stored,
the ducks return

to water – and good news,
haplessly proclaimed,
will turn to truth.

At Fifteen

I count backwards
to those awkward days
when I was just a star
on the sports teams
in that little place –
where I clamored
for space to dream –
but dreams were hostage
to the terrors of reality,
misperceived, falsely believed –
the brutal truth
beginning to appear
like a growing root
breaking through
the concrete sidewalk –
in futility, trying to hide
what had been suppressed.

I count backwards
to those awkward days
and wonder
how I survived – how
I was able to escape.
I was a hitchhiker
looking for a ride,
and my vulnerability
only made me more certain
something like a destiny
could be found –
but now I see what I was then unable
to see – the rides we find
on the lost paths to freedom

also require a fee,
and the price we pay
is the only truth we can afford.

Errand in the Wilderness

Oh Kentucky, that barren land
that enticed me before I was ready,
following a misguided dream,
a strange place that took its toll
on me, on my marriage.

That seductive period consumed
my head with theology,
paradoxical learning,
correcting faulty views of god,
shaping an epistemology for life.

But it was no place for love,
nowhere to build a lasting bond.
Living in the library, leaving only
for part-time jobs, going in debt
to make ends meet.

My young wife withered, unable
to grow in such rocky soil,
while I, submersed in Wesleyan
heritage, failed to make the deeper
issues matter, unable to make truth

out of the unintended false reality.
Poverty, immaturity, impulse,
alienation – all sublimated
with serious study, while buried
in subconsciousness, futile hope

lay – nothing but a damn cicada,
cloistered, unaware, waiting

an epoch emergence, too far in the future
to be real, some phantom life
that never was, that never could be.

Seasons of Despair

They come and they go.
Some last only the night;
some linger for days
until circumstance and will
change me, my mind
averted to other distractions
to keep me above ground.

Family is the greatest tyranny –
that old blood, as well as the new,
clouding my vision,
darkening my steps
through morning dew, walking
without hope, without direction
until finally stumbling
into meaning.

I have my fears as you have yours.
In despair I wonder what the outcome may be.
In blindness, I see my simple tragedy –
what may never be, but still the fear
of drifting aimlessly, propelled
by indifferent wind, moves me
like a dying branch unfallen.

After the fact, gratefully, I find
grace enough to land on a rocky shore,
climb a small summit
and think back on passing grief,
struggle to accept momentary relief.

But I know too well, this will not be
my last excursion into pain.
Hope, like seeds in wind,
like flowers in rain, will survive
to bloom in morning sun.

A Splatter of Rain before Daylight

Johnny Rodriguez – an old album
turns nostalgic – lost love
in two languages – something
my ex and I agreed – we liked
his music, and thirty-some years
later his coiling voice snakes
the crud out of my arteries,
hollow though stretched,
the elasticity never springing
back – the finality of fading love,
fading everything – fades
until all color is lost and the fabric
thins to something it never was –
hardly a shade of meaning –
a flimsy record of a past discarded.

Try to be understanding, feel
her desperation as you feel your own –
this aging into daylight – indifferent
as air – momentarily refreshed
by rain splattering in last moments
of darkness – its sound recurring
in the thinness of life never dying,
but never fully alive.

Life Among the Ruins

You learn to live with what's left over –
scavenging, picking your way
like an animal who only knows his appetite.

You fear the dispensation of absolute truth.
Deception abides among ruins.

You survive on half-truths, more nourishing
than anything you have found
in days gone before
or days to follow.

You wander with suspicion, find
little joys to sustain you.

You wonder, with mitigated hope,
if you can survive what really never was.

The World Bathes Tonight in Sadness

The world bathes tonight in sadness.
Bubbles float in tepid water.
I immerse myself – it seems natural.
The mind won't rest – the body,
even bones, cry in silent pain.

There's nothing to be said.
There are no words – just a feeling –
the feeling so well known,
the feeling that caresses and cradles
us like infants, wondering
how deep the water may be.

The day has been too long with me.
The night may be longer.

I envy Time. I want to be
the red bird, content, at the feeder –
its beauty complete in its limitation,
satisfied without knowing.

But for us, for me, the sadness.

Bathed in silence – sadness
made sadistic by silence.

Listen close! Hear sadness seeping,
slipping to the surface,
struggling up to where the pain –
the same old pain – feels always new.

Once I Made a God

Once I made a God
because I felt I needed something
to believe in, something to worship
like just about everyone else I meet,
and I was tired of being suspect.

So, I made a God – a combination
of male and female, but more,
and It was intimately interested
in all my fastidious failures,
laughed at my foolish flights of fancy.

Since I had made myself a God,
I sensed I should pray,
and so I did – so I did

but the bodies I saw along the road
blinded me – the gleaming
sunlight reflected from breathless teeth
visible through open mouths,
agape since the moment of death.

My made-up God could not comfort
me as I stepped past the dead,
and the dying all around me
crying out for help
were only cracked mirrors
I glanced in terror.

But I built an altar, sprinkled
it with twigs, doused it with fuel
and sat upon it –

alternatively recanting
and repeating articles of faith
evidently arising from some
Collected Unconsciousness.

The fire that consumes, struck
by the match of a hand
that once held pen and paper –
but now everything is gone –
except stars that never seem to die.

That Feral Question

To be a goose overhead
flying in formation,
sounding the morning
across dirt and grass-scattered prairie,
has its appeal
to one draped in robes of doubt,
the mortal question
never far away, never high enough
in flight – Earth-bound – dust
settled by winter rain.

Mortality is a stray cat
that surprises by its appearance,
scares you into twin impulses
of repulsion and compassion.

Wanting to rid it of suffering,
while answering questions
arising within, you involve yourself
beyond your ability to know.

Once settled in your domain,
that cat never leaves you for good,
sometimes wandering off
for supposed adventure
only to return home
to occupy your thoughts,
the imagined sense of higher purpose,
having been alerted, follows
you to your destined soil.

A swift-flying goose, governed
by instinct, or a superior being,
otherwise called human,
unable to disentangle
her constructed soul –
that feral question –

days turning in sunlight
toward night – certain to follow.

Against Remembering

Blessed are the functionally ignorant:
Those who tell themselves
there is nothing false to remember,
and thus, cannot be accountable
for that spurious period
simply called *the past*.

Despite Faulkner's considerable effort
to prove otherwise, far too many
have squelched the voice
of conscience – their only hope
of redemption squashed
by crass acts of defiance.

Just get over it they like to say,
as if memory is a speed bump
in a run-down neighborhood
where truth cannot abide.

This bizarre craving, this unnatural
clamoring to be unjustly new,
to be disconnected, deflates
the soul, dries the stream of grace,
dilutes living membrane,
reduces them to tiny, shiny
objects – counterfeit pennies,
freshly minted.

The false doctrine of revision
is poison drunk in desperation.

Truth is too dry, sticks in their throats
while their minds spin top-like,
the final turns wobbling in denial –
that longed-for state built
by the blood of the innocent,
sustained by the censored voice
of tyranny – a congress of clowns
whose pretense becomes dogma,
whose projection skews and slanders,
but whose pride – that chiefest of sins –
remains the cancer of a culture – engraved
on the tombstones of democracy.

Burning Trash

The simple ritual
lifts my spirit –
maybe my power to destroy
is perverted,
or maybe it is a primal source
of survival – once-upon-a-time
a major advance in technology
learned by unnamed ancestors
passed on to me
to purge myself, to empty
collections of trash,
accumulations
of superfluous activity
that would bury me
were it not for fire.

What goes around comes around
Etta James sings, and that
both comforts and haunts,
because I can't extinguish
thoughts with flame.
Phrases aren't paper,
and I am only the one
who strikes the match.

I watch as old Shiva destroys –
and I tremble with culpability.

A Broken Man

You can tell by the way he walks,
the way one foot is a half-step
behind the other, the slow,
almost sideways progression
with eyes turned inward,
a rough cap cocked askew
covering his brow, one hand
pocketed for safe keeping,
the other uncomfortably
dangling alongside.

I don't gawk, for I know
this man, recognize his gait,
feel his numbness, hear
the voices streaming
in his mind, his self-talk
trying to come to terms
with his conflicted life,
an awkward confluence
of past and future fomenting
these jilted moments.

A Little God

Who could believe the night
would be so short?

Darkness is longer than daylight,
yet night is a comet.

The pillow I found at dark lay
crumpled. I stretched

and crawled out of bed,
dressed, waited for light.

I opened a window, listened
for morning. Morning without sun.

I must be something like a little god
who makes days longer –

impotent power known only
to the restless.

It's a Knife-Lost Life

It's a knife-lost life –
defenseless, dull –
left only with hands
and feet to turn soil,
to grub sustenance,
grabbing existence.

You thought you'd be
something, even
exceptional, but
these days have lost
their edge.

You search gullies
for a sharp stick
green enough
to be of some use.

What Power I Have

The power I have
is a winter leaf clinging wet
to a cold branch

so far removed
from the life of a tree,
from the roots

deep in the soil
lying dormant.
There is no color.

Nothing moves through me.
Why I have not yet fallen
I cannot say.

I refuse to think I am weak.
I refuse to believe I am strong.
I live only

with the perception
of the sentimentalist,
even the death

of a leaf, a spark
in ageless fire, consumed
by its very act.

Keeping Hope Alive

Hope is a little yellow flower
opening on a sunny hillside
in May, surrounded by dew-soaked
greens and dying elms, whose
bare limbs rest the traveling birds,
their respite among decay,
a moment to sing or just sit still –
to be – in these days when life
and death contend – and the struggle
makes beauty – reminds us
of what has been,
what might be.

Thunderstorm at 5 am.

I awaken. Thunder shakes
the house. Lightning.

I make coffee and sit numbly,
listen to rainfall,
holding a ceramic mug in my palms.

Should I do something?
Should I at least read something?

One thought berates my stillness,
my inactivity, as if I am wasting breath
in this death-like trance,
this lifeless pose – a statue,
a rock, a thing.

Another thought: the splattering rain,
the breaking sky, the growl
of thunder – all this
enters me, passes through
the atmosphere of being.

Morning comes in.
I hear it like gunfire,
hear it like a distant war.

I am captured – abandoned
to the barracks of solitude
where peace is gathered
the way a sparrow pecks
at the dust.

THE ONLY SUN WE CAN KNOW

This Dream Mess

This dream mess from the ocean,
sea ugly and making mouth sounds –

the torturous irritant before death
swallows me, refutes my futile

flight in a rowboat, battered by waves
too rough, too high to navigate.

Capsized, adrift with a reconfigured oar –
survival is a matter of innovation

but the safety of shore is a long way off.
Nothing can be seen – faith feels

like mockery while the dream persists –
and the waves bellow –

the waves, the endless waves...

Revulsion

What is within me that comes
boiling to the surface,
spilling like crude oil
staining, scarring the grass?

Its dark ugliness reviling
the calm of evening,
the uneasy peace of dawn.

I've lived a lifetime with myself
splashing like a child
in shallow water, making noise
with little else to change
the equation.

I hear the dolphin circling,
rising, sucking, exhaling,
siphoning the soul of the sea,
taking in – taking out – being one
with the universe – something
I only imagine.

On the Pier at Capano Bay

Splashes in the dark surf,
moonglow on water,
solar lights along the walkway dim
in predawn blackness.

The blending of dark sky
and bright moon mixes
pleasure of the senses
with fear of feeling too much.

What we find, what we take
with us, is the difference
between mullet and redfish –
a mockingbird and the berries
on a juniper, a tree
that never seems to die.

Provision

What the sea is
to Jimenez,
you are to me.

Lover and adversary,
a friend
sometimes disguised

but more faithful
companion
than I realize

on this voyage,
taking me
to new places

transversed
by what could kill –
both life

and death move
me – with peril
and a promise.

Coffee at First Light

Lights are on in the beach house.
Someone is making coffee.

I turn to join them, but then I hear
distant voices coming my way,
unsteady steps on treated lumber,
the pier above the water,
keeping us mammals safe
to look into the dark water –
and I think about what we are not.

I think about the drive home,
how long it will be, how the coffee
will fade in a few hours.

Pleasant moments are sprinkled
with that which we would rather not
consider – like sitting under a full moon
just a little bit too chilled for comfort,
or riding in a car with cramped legs,
or writing a poem that is close,
but so far away.

What is a friend but someone who puts up
with you, makes coffee and shares it
with you, someone who greets you
in the morning as if you really matter.

It's the exchange we have that matters –
two sticks rubbing together to make
a fire – it's so primitive, but the primal
is all we have when you get down to it.

There's nothing much except for voices
in the void, laughter cutting through air.
The smell of coffee quickens the senses.
You have no choice but to get up, stretch,
say *Good Morning* – and keep moving.

Stranding

My friends on the deck overlook
the bay, catching a few lasting
moments in pleasant conversation.
Coffee cups warm their hands.
They point out a few last details,
securing memories to take home –
sounds of ducks on water, wings
in the wind, splashes, ripples,
a myriad of lights – green, red,
amber – dull beneath the perfect
moon – pure and whiter
than Lucifer – the waning presence
of night stranding darkness
above luminous water.

If the Sea has a Soul

If the sea has a soul, it is unknowable.
Salt fills the air about me,
the water around me, beneath me.

Stay Salty the sign says, and I guess
that means keep discovering,
keep venturing, don't settle –
and somehow that appeals to me

but it also seems a mystery –
a drifting away on a tide
I could never follow.

Sing to Me Ocean

Sing Ocean. Sing to me!

Sing sad water. Sing a dirge
for the surviving
whose memory of the dying
rises with every tide.

Sing Ocean. Sing to me!

Sad, salty, water sting the joy
of sun-filled days.
Moonlight is the only salve,
wondering at the breeze
passing through me, hair
beneath my cap twinges,
cigar smoke flies away –
as I must.

A heron squawks out there.
Somewhere, a mallard quacks.
Last night, darkness filled the bay
and a pelican, big as a boat,
whiter than any ghost
floated into view – haunting,
like beauty just beyond reach.

He comes and goes in secret,
an apparition that makes you doubt
everything you feel in Corpus
Christi sun – the statue of Selena
on Shoreline Drive summons
what could have been,

but never will be.

The pelican at night confirms
another reality you know nothing
of – where scenes of ghosts
write a novel never to be read,
an unsingable song – truth
beyond interpretation.

With Only His Boots and His Song

A couple upstairs packing,
the light is on two hours before sunrise.

Another one is also up. He's ready to go,
ready to see his new wife tonight.

I'm leaning against a post
on the pier overlooking the bay.
It won't take me long to pack.
I travel light these days.
Home is waiting, but nothing is urgent.

Southeast wind ruffles my hair
under my black cap locked on tight.
A cigar struggles to stay lit.
A full moon shines above us all –
those who have and those who have not.

Some might say the old moon
is trying to bring love,
but love feels far away.

I don't shrink from the moon,
but I don't understand her ways.

My young friend says moon sparkles
on the water are fishtail scales
drifting in the breeze,
and he's probably right,
since he's in love.

But I think it's something else.
It feels like tears falling
on the cheek of a lonely man
with only his boots and his song,
ready for a long drive home,
and home will be much like here –
leaning against a post looking
at a pasture, and the moon
will still be shining.

The Gulf Coast is Two Hours Behind Us

Green fields in February
traced with Live Oak
capture our view,
control imagination.

Sunny Sunday morning
without clouds,
with little traffic, the road
opens before us, pulls
us into this liminal space
between the sea
and Interstate 35.

We are happy visitants
floating through Texas.
With the dull hum of tires
and country music radio,
we journey

mile by mile.

I can't speak for my companions,
but I find the whole thing –
the journey, the landscape,
the horizon –
all one giant metaphor –
one big moment
taking us into a realm
where consciousness gains
with every curve,
every ray of February sun.

Soon we'll bend downhill
into La Grange
and feel something has happened –
atoms never at rest.

Rope

This man is like rope,
a good strong blend – twine
upon twine upon twine –
layers of unassuming strength.

Rope is present tense –
something necessary, but
it doesn't last forever.
It can be frayed, or cut off, but
that's not how the value of rope is measured.

Rope is valued by the job:
how it can lead a horse or control a steer,
how it holds a load in place,
how it keeps things from shifting,
how it makes the payload safe for transport,
how handy it is.

Rope is contemporary,
and what it delivers, what it makes possible
is its lasting value.

Rope is the product of the good Earth,
and in the right hands
nothing could be more practical,
more beneficial – nothing
could be more necessary.

The Tractor Circling

It purrs, runs so smoothly
it's almost embarrassing.
My ancestors with horses,
and then with used machinery
maintained by their ingenuity,
must think it cute to see
a greenhorn like me operating
a high-dollar rig mowing
uncontrolled Johnson Grass.

But something more than play,
something beyond power
accompanies me as I work
through stands of grass.
Something comes over me,
as I feel my nerves relax.

Nothing feels quite the same
as driving a tractor – becoming
part of the machine itself –
the cleanest, high-tech diesel
engine firing – as if I might
take flight, circle the stars
and land on the Moon.

But the Moon has no grass,
no thistle, no butterflies,
no dragonflies, nothing in the soil,
and I need this organic ritual –
to feel my boot release the clutch,
the throttle roar, the blades engage.

Gladly I settle for Earth,
the best place to garden,
to grow old and one day die –
leaving my scattered ashes
across a prairie, lifted by wind.

I pull my cap down tight,
cover my nose with a red bandanna,
work in solitude – save the hawks
above me – circling.

Digging Deep

Find the roots below the surface,
the source of everything.
Avoid the superficial.

Too much of everything
is surface – glib, false humor,
trite expressions,
the veneer of pretense,
mock happiness,
an extended lie.

Dig deep below the surface.
Find the roots,
the source of everything.

Why? The jaded asks –
the pompous playboy,
the dull procrastinator,
the poser who says he's an artist,
who undresses himself in public
to be seen – grasping attention
where there's nothing to offer.

Avoid the parade of charades
by those who would steal your heart.

Dig deep to find your soul
buried below the nutritious soil
covered with weedy grass,
layers upon layers.

The root travels down,

inward, connects to itself –
buried in the hope of eternal return,
hidden in unmovable security.

The world is held together by roots.

What we see above ground
is just the growth springing
from that hidden source.
What we hear above ground
is a template waiting
to be transcribed,
the novella of the self –
dusty, precious, unremarkable
but beyond comprehension.

Find the hidden source.
Know the depths –
only then will joy emerge,
only then can something
called happiness prevail,
only then can anger be redeemed,
only then can disappointment
serve you, and help others,
only then can love be true.

Elegy for a Former Student

Every day, coming
and going, I pass over
the spot that took her life –
even after two years
the highway is scarred
where she was hit head-on.

Her unborn baby was delivered
by the miracle of science,
flying by helicopter in the womb
of a dying mother.

What a story the child
will one day learn –
what a senseless tragedy
that keeps me safely
in my lane, driving
to meet so many students
who also have their private grief,
lingering, sometimes festering,
while the explication
of literature continues –
challenging us all
to grasp what beauty,
what truth
we can,
while we can.

On a Hillside Near Eureka Springs

Dark settles among pine trees
and brown-leafed oak.
I look out into the slimmest sky,
just enough light to see an owl
flapping through dusk.

It's quiet, except for the occasional car.

I know no one here, and no one knows me
and there's not much to the evening
except to think about the disappointing day,
a day built up in my expectation – yet now I see
there was no real basis for my anticipation,
just hope glimmering in the March breeze –
and now, facing the anticlimactic,
with its restless summons I must answer,
a return to the gritty routine of my tomorrows.

But before that, before tomorrow comes,
tonight, without celebration, I sit on this hillside,
look through dark pines into sky closing in
on me, hear wind-rustled leaves, wonder how far
that owl flew, imagine where it landed –
some isolated branch, no doubt.

The Uninvited Known

I know some things
  I should not know
and that makes me feel
  important.

Like hummingbirds
  at the feeder
fighting for a place
  in small sky

my mind recalls
  what I have seen
and what I have heard,
  what I was.

Wings of knowing
  pound the air at dusk
restless, without resolve,
  just buzzing

in frantic flight,
  holding still just long enough
to taste the providence
  of sugar

mixed in water,
  a quick fearful sip,
suspended in air, then
  off I go

in manic flight.
  What am I to do

with what I know? This
   found burden

doesn't slow me
   but fuels more flight,
a paradox that wrinkles
   anxious sheets

in the dark night,
   turning this way and that,
my body recoiling in heat,
   or shivered

with knees up-tucked,
   trying to hide from life,
burrowed in a lair, to not
   remember.

When morning seeps
   through faded curtains,
I look for something familiar
   but I know

light is a guise
   and hope is a seldom high
only known until I resolve to
   try again

to make something
   happen new. With cautious
promise I rise and stretch
   my body

rub sleep-marked eyes,
   sense appetite, and for a time
I am distracted. My body

draws me out.

A crusted shell,
   now I am a moth emerging,
obeying what light I have
   escaping

layers of night.
   But I know in a few hours
my mind will reassert itself and
   the cycle

of displacing
   the uninvited known will return.
I look for tasks of denial
   to be free

from what I know.
   I think of praying, a phrase
or two comes to mind
   to survive
the fallenness felt.
   I cling to forgiveness, setting
the labored self aside
   to make it

through awareness
   with acceptable performance,
obedient to duty as I
   understand it.

This layered self
   moves me like a train,
powerless except for the track
   I follow.

I'm divided.
   Like a river splitting two ways
that never seems to unite,
   the streaming

makes its own way,
   my own private course
followed, cutting the banks
   of fresh soil

that feels so much
   the same. I tell myself
to go on, put it out of my mind
   for a while.

Cursed with knowing,
   the importance has been lost.
I envy tree frogs. I hear
   the coyotes

gather, crying,
   their tragic voices blending
in desperation under
   a half-moon

and I am moved.
   Their plaintiff chorus hanging

in the breeze – the eternity
   of the wind.

Keep Mortality in Mind

When sunset feels compromised
and sunrise adds nothing but reminders
of selfishness, like gulls clamoring
for crumbs on a littered beach –
when underappreciated, overworked,
suspicioned, taken for granted –
when Diogenes' flame is extinguished
by careless breath – when attempts at art
become a sideshow – when fantasies
of heaven and rumors of hell only
disappoint and dissuade commonsense –
then, keep mortality in mind – soon
you will be dead, and all will be fine.

Thoughts on the Soul

If we call it soul,
and if by that
we mean without substance
but not without meaning,
not without an inner life,
a light – maybe a lantern's
flickering flame
in a dark, windy night –
tremulous but not timid.

Brave, but beautiful?

An ugly soul lives, too,
moves in darkness,
sinister, incinerate,
seeking to destroy,
ignited by its own
debilitating source,
fueled by the evil
that floats about us.

Guard the soul!

Take care of your light.
Not everything that glows
redeems, not everything
that shines seeks to heal,
to restore, to warm us,
to warn us.

Only in irony, only
with tested perception

can we know.

What we find out
is often too late to fix.

The heart is deceitful
and desperately wicked.
Who can know it?

The Silence of Eternity

In silence before human breath,
trees stand tall in dim light.
The wind has yet to rise.
Morning drizzle covers the land,
a soggy portent, but none can see
its outcome, intended or not.

In the middle of Time, creation
becomes crowded with clamoring minds,
august proclamation, deceptive hearts.

The race hunts, gathers, then farms.
It builds the thing called civilization
but fails to see the end of its purpose –
destruction so brutally enslaved
until death, its only recourse, mocked
by tragic words, falls into an abyss
of its own making.

And silence returns –
and the thing called God, ruling
without end or beginning,
in quietude.

The stars above, the soil below,
in conspiratorial gesture, speak
the only words remaining,
too often, unheard...

The Source of Liberty

The sky goes up forever.
The sky goes on forever,
interrupted only by trees
on hills on the horizon
shaping my existence.

The sky is pale blue.
The sun is far away.
Tonight, Jupiter will hang close
to the moon and I will sing
a silent song, praise that rises
within me, and freedom
rushes toward me,
from seemingly nowhere,
consuming me.

In the morning, the horizon
will beckon, and I will follow,
walk across ancient land,
curved, crisp contours
intermediating endless sky
and bonds I may yet escape.

One day, clouds will form,
softly at first, then tighten
like a fist, and pummel
the land with dark rain,
and for a while darkness
will again cover the Earth
as in the beginning.

But the memory of blue sky,
with its secret eternity,
will stay with me, will color
me while I wait the return
of light – the fresh smell
of nourished soil, rainwater
seeping the surface
of vegetation then sinking
below summer ground.

Freedom is found in this cycle.
Liberty lies deep in the soul,
lingers in the heart of the soil.
Something in the sky
and timeless in dirt, quickens
me, makes me rise up
and walk into light.

When Time Comes Calling

I'm sure when Time comes calling
I will be crawling back to faith
since my uncertain rebellion
will not have vanquished fear,
and fear betrays courage,
and doubt lingers like evergreens
never dead, but alive only with staid
conformity.

My return to my knees
must accompany a regression
toward irksome sincerity –
I believe – because emotion
rules intellect.

My proud, upright pilgrimage
with discernment leads only
to the hope of regaining hope.

It does, after all, seem safer
to crawl across the floor.
Striving, or even standing,
invites terror.
Mind over Matter
is meaningless.

I imagine I want to be cradled
in Mother Church,
protected, if not loved,
by the very force I have feared.

But congregationalism
is tribalism – the politicizing
of faith obstructs my path,
even on my knees.

Can I love that which obdurate
believers love, and not be
one of them?

Can I obey evil mandates
masked in righteous zeal?

Can faith blossom in winter
isolation any more than a songbird
can survive pecking seeds
off a frozen yard?

And the hawk is never far away.

Though faith finds a few seeds
graciously scattered,
can the solitary bird expect
to retain purpose
other than fulfilling a role –
whether drab-feathered
or bright as a Cardinal –
a suspicious role assigned
by an unknowable force
that permits, even demands,
a few songs in a short life?

When Time comes calling
will my crawling toward faith
be enough?

Where is the mother to watch

over me, to clear my path?
Does the crawling infant
even know its parents?

The bird in winter,
a man on his knees,
what more certain truth can render
the luckless lives of these?

A Remembered Sun

Rain. Gray sky.
Dripping sounds
and the sun's feebleness
feels forlorn, fettering
us with green leaves,
gorging grass.

We flounder through dank,
dark days – time
pauses, pulses slow –
we trudge web-footed
through the yard, conjure
a remembered sun.

The only way to be
is to become less
than once imagined,
be our own light –
at times, the only sun
we can know.

Acknowledgments

The Peace that Morning Brings was written for the marriage of Debbie and Chris Whitesides

Born Under a Full Moon was written at the birth of grandson Arlo Wren Hada

Rivers is dedicated to Casey Saunders

Sisters is dedicated to Kai Coggin

Keeping Hope Alive is dedicated to Mark Walling

A Strange Weed and *Rope* are dedicated to Paul Bowers

Digging Deep is for all the students I've been privileged to know

~

These poems first appear in the following journals:

Thunder Sounds Morning Sky Alive, *Amethyst Review*
This Miraculous World, *San Pedro River Review*

About the Author

Ken Hada lives and writes in the Crosstimbers in Pottawatomie County, Oklahoma. He enjoys presenting his work at venues across the country. His *Contour Feathers* received the Oklahoma Book Award. *Bring an Extry Mule* won the SCMLA Prize for Poetry; *Spare Parts* received the Wrangler Award from the National Western Heritage Museum. *Visions for the Night* is his twelfth full-length collection. More at kenhada.org.